Why is it that anyone willing to wear the costume is eligible for the job? And why do we encourage our kids to sit in a bearded stranger's lap and share their deepest wishes, while we spend the rest of the year instructing them to stay away from these people? You have to admit, it's a little weird.

"Perhaps the most unsettling batch of holiday pictures ever compiled."
—Time.com

"An *awesome* new holiday tradition, one in which terrifying men who dress as Kris Kringle for Christmas are mocked for their creepiness."
—The Huffington Post

"Sometimes a co-worker uncovers something so magical, so special, that it requires the entire office to stop and marvel in awe of its viral glory. This year, we have Sketchy Santas."
—Trendhunter

". . . Will have you laughing all the way thr[...]"
—MTV.com

W W W . S K E T C H Y S A N T A S . [...]

818.602
Z

GALLERY
BOOKS

New York

London

Toronto

Sydney

SKETCHY SANTAS

A Lighter Look at the Darker Side of St. Nick

• • •

WILL ZWEIGART

Gallery Books
A Division of Simon & Schuster, Inc.
1230 Avenue of the Americas
New York, NY 10020

First Gallery Books trade paperback edition November 2010

GALLERY BOOKS and colophon are trademarks of Simon & Schuster, Inc.

For information about special discounts for bulk purchases, please contact Simon & Schuster Special Sales at 1-866-506-1949 or business@simonandschuster.com.

The Simon & Schuster Speakers Bureau can bring authors to your live event. For more information or to book an event contact the Simon & Schuster Speakers Bureau at 1-866-248-3049 or visit our website at www.simonspeakers.com.

Designed by Jaime Putorti
Background art from istockphoto.com

Manufactured in the United States of America

10   9   8   7   6   5   4   3   2   1

Library of Congress Cataloging-in-Publication Data is available.

ISBN 978-1-4391-9760-8
ISBN 978-1-4391-9761-5 (ebook)

AUTHOR'S NOTE

This book is intended solely as humorous commentary based on my looking at these photographs alone—it's all in good fun. I do not have any personal knowledge regarding any of the Santas or any other individuals depicted, and none of the statements in this book are intended to be understood as true or as factual allegations. All quotations attributed to Santa or any other individual depicted in this book are entirely my invention. In other words, all my quips are supposed to be funny jokes intended to make the reader smile and should not be taken seriously at all.

CONTENTS

INTRODUCTION

Santa Claus has captured our imaginations for centuries as an enduring symbol of kindness and generosity. A beloved mythical figure who brings joy to kids everywhere, he's a beacon of hope for children across the world—part confidant, part gift-bearing superhero. But with great power comes great responsibility.

So why is it that anyone willing to wear the costume is eligible for the job? And why do we encourage our kids to sit in a bearded stranger's lap and share their deepest wishes, while we spend the rest of the year instructing them to stay away from these people? You have to admit, it's a little weird.

These days just about any guy with a red suit, a fake beard, and a few hours to kill can become St. Nick. And that's the problem, really—there's no quality control. It's not surprising that, for many of us, time spent on Santa's lap has been anything but joyful.

This book is a collection of photographs featuring our favorite holiday hero in a variety of compromising positions. These images may force you to look more closely at the man in red and white, and question one of our time-honored shopping mall traditions.

Why are certain Santas so sketchy, you ask? How did they come to be this way? What are some helpful tips for identifying them? This book will answer those

questions—but let's get a few things straight before we begin.

WE ARE NOT HERE TO JUDGE.

———

To any professional Santas out there who might take offense at the title of this book, I would say, "Whoa, sir. Whoa," with my hands facing outward in a calming manner. I'm not here to point fingers. And I'm certainly not suggesting that *every* Santa is *actually* sketchy. We've all had photos snapped at inopportune moments. We don't necessarily think they say anything about your appearance at any other moment, but they're all we have! This is just a celebration of those moments—a roast, if you will—where we look at

funny photos, talk about how great you guys are, and make a few jokes at your expense. Do you know how awesome you have to be to even deserve a roast? As far as you know, we're laughing *with* you, not at you.

STRANGE LAPS ARE SKETCHY BY NATURE.

There's nothing more comforting for kids than climbing into their parents' laps—it's a totally natural and healthy thing to do. But being dropped onto a stranger's lap is scary, which makes it more fun for camera-happy parents. (Hey, if you can't laugh at your own kids, who can you laugh at?)

WE KNOW IT'S TOUGH OUT THERE.

Being Santa is no doubt a really hard job. You're surrounded by strangers, flashing cameras, weird smells (some of them emanating from your own rental suit), middle-aged elves, and screaming kids. You probably feel like an ass holding down kids who want to run away, and when they tug on your beard or pee in your lap you have to smile, even when you're really frowning inside.

So to you, dearest Santa, we express our most sincere gratitude. Thanks for filling the world with holiday cheer, and for letting everybody hang out in your warm lap beneath your bacon-scented beard.

Please join us in a toast (and a roast) as we raise our flasks to Sketchy Santas everywhere.

You Better Watch Out

It seems that Santa may be losing control of his "personal brand." Every December there are news stories about Santa Claus robbing a bank, getting a DUI, or violating his probation. Even worse, convicted sex offenders are sometimes found out and fired from their jobs as mall Santas. Many cities around the world host annual Santa pub crawls, where inebriated hoards dressed in red suits gather to engage in various shenanigans.

I even googled "Santa Claus Porn"—you know, just

to see how deep the depravity runs—and was amazed to find more than 800,000 results. I spent hours and hours closely investigating each one of these sites (with disgust) until the library asked me to leave. Do you remember how you felt when you found out Santa Claus wasn't real? Imagine stumbling upon a video called "Christmas in July," where the main character's name is July, and Santa's wearing assless chaps.

Yet despite all this, parents still willingly line up to plop their tots in a strange man's lap. We owe it to ourselves—nay, our children—to take a closer look at how this all started.

A Background Check on Santa Claus

T hings began innocently enough in fourth-century Turkey, when a wealthy bishop named St. Nicholas became legendary for helping other people. He gave alms to the poor, saved women from being sold into prostitution, and even protected baby seals from pirates (the latter is unconfirmed). His signature move was donating gifts late at night, when fewer people were likely to be around, which made it easier to protect his anonymity. Soon parents started sending their kids to bed early with the warning that he would only come when they were asleep.

Long after St. Nick's death, word of his good deeds (also known as "solids" back then) spread throughout Europe. The Dutch called him "Sinterklass" and began celebrating his feast day (December 6) by giving gifts and high-fives to one another. They carried this tradition to New York City, where he was dubbed the city's patron saint. By the 1820s, Christmas gift-giving had "gone viral," and retail stores were beginning to get in on the action.

Around this time, Santa was looking to reinvent himself as more fun-loving and commercially viable. He got his first paid gig in 1841, when a Philadelphia department store hired him to climb the chimney and just "hang out" in order to show children that he was

real. While his saintly robes were gone, this version of St. Nick seemed more charismatic and jolly. (Maybe that was a result of the booze?) Kids responded favorably to his new look, and pretty soon public appearances were in high demand.

Over the next few decades, Santa became a leading spokesman for the holiday retail industry. He partnered with leading soft drink and cigarette manufacturers for lucrative print and TV campaigns. He enjoyed the spoils of being the first American superstar—parades, film, music, merchandise, and a limitless supply of milk and cookies. But we all know what happens when celebrities get a little too big, too fast. Pretty soon Santa was showing signs of excess. His waistline

Gifts that say *Merry Christmas* with every puff...

Camel

Camel

Camel

Camel *Cigarettes*

Prince Albert *Smoking Tobacco*

9

ballooned, and when he did show up to gigs, he was often completely trashed (no thanks to his red-nosed enabler and drinking buddy, Rudolph).

By the early 1900s, Santa seemed to be everywhere—and, in fact, he was. In order to meet the increasing demand, he began to "franchise" himself with thousands of look-alikes, an army of bearded clones out to spread the good word of retail-driven generosity. But rather than question his sudden ubiquity, Americans embraced it. They liked having the guy around. And more Santas meant more sales at the mall and more donations for charities.

While this became quite a boon to the transient part-time labor force, it also created some "quality assurance" issues, to put things delicately. Somewhere along this path of explosive expansion, we lost sight of the characteristics that made Santa such a great guy in the first place.

WHEN THE SANTAS COME MARCHING IN

Today things seem to be under control at your average shopping mall . . . for the most part.

Does that mean Sketchy Santas are an endangered species? Far from it. Cleanse the malls, and they will flee to budget day care and senior centers. Sweep the streets and they will hide in their vans or mobilize flash-mob bar crawls in trendy urban areas. Disturbingly, large pockets of "Santarchists" are sprouting

up all over the world. They say it's not a movement (that's something you do in the bathroom), but their numbers are growing at an alarming rate.

Is the Santa Claus brand being hijacked by a shiftless gang of drunks and misfit revelers? Is his legacy as a generous, kindly saint in jeopardy? Only time will tell, but one thing is certain— we must be vigilant.

A Field Guide to

SKETCHY SANTAS

With nearly 50,000 malls and shopping centers in the United States alone, there will never be enough "authentic" Santas to go around every year. I've developed a simple model—let's call it the Sketchy Curve—to illustrate this point.

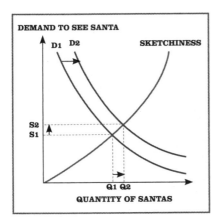

A balance between the number of Santas available and a parent's desire to have their children see St. Nick in a timely manner loosely determines the potential sketchiness of Santas in your area. As demand (D) increases, you can expect a corresponding increase in quantity (Q) of available Santas and the sketchiness (S) of any given Santa.

Now that we all understand the statistical inevitability of some shady dudes slipping through the cracks, what can be done about it? This book is your best defense. Start by closely reviewing the following chapters for possible indications that your Santa may be sketchy.

Excessive
Inebriation

Bourbon doesn't hide itself well on the breath—even behind beef jerky—so this is probably the easiest way to tell if your Santa should be sleeping one off instead of stumbling out of his sleigh. Hangovers and kids don't mix well before noon, either—so cut these guys some slack.

"Don't judge me, kid—it's noon somewhere."

Just before Tara snuck down to find presents, looks like Santa found the schnapps.

Santa is a master multitasker:
His good eye never left the
eggnog bowl.

Maybe Kim just loves the smell of cheap gin and venison in the morning.

The original
Weekend at Bernie's . . .

"Are you seriously mocking me? Your brother thinks he's Shaun Cassidy—why don't you mock him instead!"

27

"Oh, hell no."

"It's cool if I chain-smoke around
the kid, right?"

"Welcome to Margaritaville, kid. I'll get you that Malibu Barbie if you help me find my lost shaker of salt."

"Mom, I think he needs his diaper changed!"

"Guys, if you're serious about this bank heist, we're going to need a wheelman and more muscle."

32

"Gimme the keys, Santa—
I'll drive. . . ."

"What are these brats crying about?
I've been getting peed on since noon
and you don't see me bawling."

"Kid, if it ain't Kentucky
white lightning, it ain't 'shine."

"Just because Santa can't feel his face doesn't mean he can't feel your insults."

"Now don't be alarmed . . . but one of my elves over there has a kni— don't all look at once!"

"If I weren't napping right now,
I'd really give you something
to cry about. . . ."

As Santa nodded off, Garrett
saw his opportunity for escape.

WARDROBE
MALFUNCTIONS

When Santa doesn't dress the part, it's a less-than-subtle way of saying he just doesn't give a damn. Face tattoos, white paint, and excessive use of eyeliner can all be considered reliable indicators that things will go downhill quickly.

"Some thirsty vampire puts on a Santa Claus costume and you just . . . hand me over?"

Escaped convict from the burn ward? Or just Grandmother?

"Come on, sis, a transvestite-clown-Santa! Don't be such a stick in the mud—just go with it!"

This was before background checks, psychotherapy, and stain remover.

Dad achieves "fourth-quarter holiday efficiencies" by dressing as Ghost Santa.

45

Did you know the phrase
"saved by the bell" originated
in Poland?

"So what if I wear a little guyliner? It really makes my eyes pop in photographs."

"I promise not to cry if you tell me where you got this kick-ass beard."

"Turned my teardrop tat into a bat 'cause kids like animals and shit."

"This year, you sit on *my* lap!"

It seemed like a good idea not to mention the mustache.

"Ma, you can coax all you want—
I am not sitting on that man's lap.
He's three-quarters beard!"

"This mustache glue smells incredible—I've gone through half a tube just this morning!"

"Smile, Braceface, and let's get this over with—it's 500 degrees in this suit."

As the mob rushed in, Santa needed to make a quick decision—defend the presents, or escape with his life.

When Santa's embarrassed to
be photographed with you,
it's time to change.

"We're rolling now?
No hair and makeup?"

"Seriously, who dresses you kids?"

"All I want for Christmas is anything but a leisure suit. . . ."

"Hold still, I gotta practice my ventriloquism bit."

Maybe it was his breasts, or the spaghetti beard, but something was off.

"Santa! Is that a Mr. T action figure in your pocket?"

Things went downhill quickly after
Santa sneezed his beard off.

63

"Just grin and bear it, Charles."

"Can we speed this up a little bit?"

PET PEEVES

Wait a minute—who actually takes their pet to the mall? Santa gets a pass on this one. He's already got enough mystery stains without having to hold an incontinent shih tzu.

"This hold is called the 'cat nap.'"

"Can anyone tell I have puppies
stuffed under my shirt?
Room for one more?"

Squirt, Chaps, and Cha Chi
all agreed: If anybody has bacon,
it's this guy.

Just bide your time, Rupert. This muzzle's coming off at some point, and then they'll get theirs. All of them.

"You can rub my belly and flash those smoky eyes all you want, Grinch— I am not going to wear those antlers."

Guess whose breath smells better.

Off-site
Locations

Mall too crowded? Rogue, second-tier Santas can be found in the most unlikely of places. Just stay alert and always have an emergency exit plan.

"Santa, what did that man mean
by 'ritual sacrifice'?"

Bench Santa's just a little down on his luck.

"First rule of Mall Santa Fight Club:
You do not talk about Mall
Santa Fight Club."

"Pizza party at Santa's apartment later!"

Clutching the tiniest of candy canes in her right hand, Sarah wondered how she could have been lured into Santa's lap so easily.

Janitor Santa gives
the worst presents.

Displaying an early flair for unnecessary drama, Martin bravely pledged all of his presents to charity should he not return.

"I'll just stand, thanks."

Only the most well-behaved children get an invitation to Santa's closet.

"Why trek all the way to the mall when there's a Santa living in your basement?"

"Well this has been great, Santa—
but Mom says you can't sleep on
our couch anymore."

"Comrade, I am legitimate Santa Claus. I insist you will comply immediately."

"I said Santa Claus, not the Gorton's fisherman, you idiot! Screw it—just help me get these kids in the van!"

"No flash photography!"

"He smells like Grandpa's bedpan."

89

JUST PLAIN EVIL

What's that mysterious foam around his mouth—rabies or spray cheese? What's he whispering underneath that noticeably unpleasant breath? That's why it's fun, people—you never really know.

"Run! He'll drink your soul!"

Santa let Margie in on his secret . . . let's just say she didn't take it all that well. And Bobby . . . Bobby doesn't give a shit about anything.

"Goddamn double shift at The Home Depot and now this shit."

What Tony remembers most are the smells—mothballs, pudding, women's perfume, and death.

"Get Elmo out of my face and put me down! You're wrinkling the Burberry!"

"The harder you cry,
the harder I squeeze."

"Go ahead, scream as loud as you want—Santa can't hear high frequencies."

After his first three escape attempts failed, Josiah began to pee his way out.

Finally, Bizzaro Santa Claus found a willing protégé to do his evil bidding . . . bwahahahahaha!

Amy can't believe she fell for
the giant Snoopy trap—

twice!

"I can't un-fart, kid. It's already out there, so just deal with it."

"Santa's going to put these little hands to work up North."

We'll never know what Santa whispered in Samantha's ear.

She hasn't spoken since.

"Do not, under any circumstances, stop smiling until Christmas. And I see you when you're sleeping, so that counts, too."

"Sing it, Baby Gaga!"

"I need an adult! I mean,
another adult!"

NEVER
TOO OLD

Sometimes Santa just needs to be with people his own age, people who won't tug on his ear and wipe snot on his sleeve. People who can *hug back*.

When you get too old for the lap, there's always "the awkward prom pose."

"Nothing beats hanging out in the break room in my long johns and getting a free lap dance from Betty in HR. . . ."

Um. No comment.

Santa's behavior had been raising eyebrows all day.

"I'll send you a poke request on MyFace, or whatever they call it."

Patrick and Devin's
Not-So-Excellent Lap Adventure

"You mind if I get some extra copies of this photo?"

"I don't care how many candy
canes this guy is offering—
we're done here."

THOSE EYES

Avoid making direct eye contact with Santa if he seems a little "off." You have no idea what kinds of strange chemicals and/or processed meat products might be coursing through his system, so pose for your photo quickly and retreat to the safety of a nearby Orange Julius.

Maybe Santa has a little score to settle
with the photographer. Maybe he'll be
waiting in the parking lot later.

"Man, Alabama Santas suck."

"Let's see if I can call this one:
You're all going to get
hand-me-downs. And lice."

123

Santa's crying, too. Inside.

"Your lame stories are putting me to sleep, kid. Let's wrap this up."

"Laugh, and the world laughs with you; whine, and you're on your own."

"Can we swap this one out?
I think it's leaking."

"Remember, Santa's keeping an eye on you."

"Just stay away from the bottle,
the bookies, and the hookers,
and you'll go far."

129

"And that, my young friends,
is what they call 'silent but deadly.'"

"Why so serious?"

"Keep digging in that bag of presents, Santa—the one you're holding is too small to be a Barbie Dream House."

"Fruit? I'm getting a baggie full of fruit for Christmas? You've got to be shitting me."

"Okay, low budget, I get it—but how about a freakin' chair? I can't hold two kids and squat here all day."

Sean was born to run . . .
which might come in handy sooner
than he realizes.

"Sure, I'll loan you my white gloves, Susie . . . right after I wad them up and stuff them in your brother's mouth."

"Jesus, Blitzen, what's the missus been feeding you—vindaloo?"

52750

"I need a raise and a single malt,
not necessarily in that order."

"If you want any presents this year,
go tell that mall security guard
he's a poopy head."

"Be a good girl like your big sister
or I'll shove that candy cane
up your nose."

"Ever actually tried taking candy from a baby? It's pretty awesome."

141

"Hands off the Cabbage Patch, please."

143

A LITTLE TOO JOLLY

Somewhere between the occasional good-natured chuckle and a constant, earsplitting roar lies the delicate balance of Santa's sanity. If he's loitering in the mall parking lot and asking strangers to jingle his bells, notify mall security.

Sure, Elliot was displeased,
but the all-you-can-eat lollipop deal
was simply unbeatable.

Older siblings enjoy many
privileges during the holidays;
none sweeter than this.

St. Nick or old hippie biker?
You decide.

"Now you tickle me, Elmo."

There's no shame in weeping openly after being restrained by a large man wearing white gloves.

Tammy was, in fact, ticklish—
she just didn't want to give Santa
the satisfaction.

"Just breathe through your mouth,"
Lindsay told herself.

"Jump! You can make it!"

"Reeeeeeach!"

"We're all out of presents,
so here's a foot rub."

With everyone fooled by the old "look over there" trick, Samantha proceeded to strangle her brother with his own overalls.

"Mom, you really don't see any
red flags here? Come on.
Shut it down."

"Donner! Get off Vixen right now! Not okay, guys, not okay!"

"I told you—I already went through security!"

If he squeezes any harder,
Colleen will be leaving Santa
a present.

CONCLUSION

We've taken a closer look at Santa's meteoric rise from anonymous saint to global hero. We've shown how his personal brand began to erode over time as more malls and shopping centers demanded someone—anyone—with a red suit and a beard. We've even provided a handy field guide for identifying potential Sketchy Santas in your neighborhood.

The only thing left to do is ask ourselves: *Would we really have it any other way?*

Sketchy Santas have become a part of our traditions, our memories, and who we are. Parents work so hard to give their kids a perfect Christmas, but as any classic holiday movie shows (pick your favorite), it never really works out that way. Inevitably there will be drama, alcohol, tears, and the occasional awkward embrace.

That's why these "visits with Santa" are an early metaphor for the holiday experiences we'll have later in life—sometimes flawed, but always special. If everything about Christmas were perfect, it wouldn't be so memorable.

Do we really care about authenticity anyway?

Our interpretation of Santa has always been an ever-changing mashup of dozens of different cultures, folk stories, commercial interpretations, and conflicting ideas. Santas vary by gender, ethnicity, geography, budget, and waistline. Even if there was a universally accepted version (which sounds kind of boring)—so what?

It's about the *idea* of Santa, not the man. He is whoever we want him to be—and there's a little Sketchy Santa in all of us.

Merry Christmas everyone.

GOOD-BYE ALL

ACKNOWLEDGMENTS

First and most importantly, a huge thanks to everyone who submitted their photos for SketchySantas.com. You found the courage to share your sketchiest memories with the world—and this book proves you are not alone!

To the team at Gallery Books—especially Kate Dresser and my amazing editor, Tricia Boczkowski—who found themselves involuntarily dreaming about Sketchy Santas all summer. Hope this doesn't ruin Christmas forever for you guys.

To my agent—Lindsay Edgecombe at Levine Greenberg—for her endless patience, persistence, and professionalism. It's been such a pleasure to work with you.

To my brother, Warren, and Tom and Nancy Zweigart—the best parents anyone could ever ask for. Thanks for braving many long lines to see Santa throughout the years, even when I chickened out and ran away at the last minute.

To my Google Chat editorial support team—particularly Lindsey Weber, Alex Blagg, "Carles" from HipsterRunoff.com, and the entire Urlesque.com meme squad. Thanks, bros.

Lastly, I offer my most sincere gratitude to Colleen Phelan. Thanks for your unconditional love and support.

PHOTO CREDITS